CW00932944

SPORTS' GREATEST TURNAROUNDS

BY HEATHER RULE

THE WILD WORLD OF SPORTS

SportsZone

An Imprint of Abdo Publishing
abdopublishing.com

abdopublishing.com

Published by Abdo Publishing, a division of ABDO, PO Box 398166, Minneapolis, Minnesota 55439. Copyright © 2018 by Abdo Consulting Group, Inc. International copyrights reserved in all countries. No part of this book may be reproduced in any form without written permission from the publisher. SportsZone™ is a trademark and logo of Abdo Publishing.

Printed in the United States of America, North Mankato, Minnesota
102017
012018

THIS BOOK CONTAINS
RECYCLED MATERIALS

Cover Photos: James Marsh/BPI/Rex Features/AP Images, foreground; Mark Duncan/AP Images, background
Interior Photos: Ron Frehm/AP Images, 5; AP Images, 6–7; Tsugufumi Matsumoto/AP Images, 8; Jim Mone/AP Images, 11, 12; Dave Martin/AP Images, 15; Allen Kee/AP Images, 17; Adam Butler/AP Images, 19; Andrew Cohoon/AP Images, 20–21; Paul Warner/AP Images, 23, 25; Tom Pidgeon/Getty Images Sport/Getty Images, 24; Amy Sancetta/AP Images, 27; Kathy Willens/AP Images, 28; Ann Heisenfelt/AP Images, 31; Ryan Remiorz/Canadian Press/AP Images, 32–33; Winslow Townson/AP Images, 34; Charles Krupa/AP Images, 37; TGSPhoto/Rex Features/AP Images, 39; Matt Dunham/AP Images, 40; Kyodo/AP Images, 42; David J. Phillip/AP Images, 45

Editor: Patrick Donnelly
Series Designer: Craig Hinton

Publisher's Cataloging-in-Publication Data

Names: Rule, Heather, author.
Title: Sports' greatest turnarounds / by Heather Rule.
Description: Minneapolis, Minnesota : Abdo Publishing, 2018. | Series: The wild world of sports | Includes online resources and index.
Identifiers: LCCN 2017946936 | ISBN 9781532113673 (lib.bdg.) | ISBN 9781532152559 (ebook)
Subjects: LCSH: Sports comebacks--Juvenile literature. | Sports--Miscellanea--Juvenile literature. | Sports--United States--History--Juvenile literature.
Classification: DDC 796--dc23
LC record available at https://lccn.loc.gov/2017946936

TABLE OF
CONTENTS

MIRACLE METS

New York Mets first baseman Marv Throneberry hit a triple against the Chicago Cubs in 1962. But he was called out because he didn't touch second base. He didn't touch first base, either. It's no wonder Casey Stengel, manager of those 1962 Mets, famously asked, "Can't anybody here play this game?"

The Mets joined the National League (NL) in 1962 and lost a modern-day-record 120 games in their first season. That wasn't really a fluke. They lost more than 100 games in five of their first six seasons. They were so bad that they never spent even one day in first place.

Then came 1969. The "Amazin' Mets" rattled off 11 wins in a row, putting them in second place in early June. They stayed there for three months before passing the Chicago Cubs in September in the midst of a 10-game winning streak. The team that couldn't get it right for most of the decade was suddenly unbeatable.

Jerry Koosman won 17 games for the Mets in 1969.

From left, infielder Ed Charles, Koosman, and catcher Jerry Grote celebrate after the Mets finished off the Orioles in the 1969 World Series.

The Mets finished 100–62, champions of the NL East Division. They swept the NL West champion Atlanta Braves in the playoffs. That set up a showdown with the mighty Baltimore Orioles in the World Series. The American League (AL) champs had won 109 games that season. Baltimore won the first game. But the Amazin' Mets didn't travel that far to come up short.

Jerry Koosman took a no-hitter into the seventh inning of Game 2, one of his two victories in the World Series for the Mets. Gary Gentry and Nolan Ryan combined for a shutout in Game 3. Ron Swoboda's run-scoring double in the eighth inning put the Mets on top in Game 5. And when left fielder Cleon Jones settled under a fly ball for the final out, the Mets had completed their miracle.

TOM TERRIFIC

Mets ace pitcher Tom Seaver tossed a near-perfect game on July 9, 1969, against the Cubs at New York's Shea Stadium. Seaver struck out 11 batters and walked none in the 4–0 victory. Rookie Jimmy Qualls singled with one out in the ninth to break up the perfect game. Seaver went on to win the NL Cy Young Award that year, posting a record of 25–7 with a 2.21 ERA.

TAKING DOWN TYSON

Sometimes a team will come out of nowhere to win a championship. But it can happen for individual athletes, too. In 1990 boxer James "Buster" Douglas was a 29-year-old journeyman with an unimpressive 29–4–1 pro record. Many boxing fans had never heard of him when it was announced that he would fight heavyweight champion Mike Tyson in Tokyo, Japan.

Tyson was the most feared boxer of his generation. He dominated his opponents, winning many matches in the first round. He brought a record of 37–0 with 33 knockouts into the ring that night in Tokyo. Experts predicted another easy victory for Tyson.

But Douglas was ready. He seemed to have more energy than Tyson, whose left eye became more swollen as the match went on. In the 10th round, Douglas threw five quick punches that sent the champion to the mat. Tyson had never been knocked down as a pro fighter. And he wasn't able to get up. It was a knockout for Douglas. The unknown boxer was the new heavyweight champion.

Buster Douglas stands over a fallen Mike Tyson after delivering the final punch of their heavyweight title bout in 1990.

WORST-TO-FIRST
WORLD SERIES

Minnesota Twins center fielder Kirby Puckett stepped to the plate in the bottom of the 11th inning. With the score tied, the stocky slugger waited for his pitch. And when he got it, he blasted it into the left-field seats.

Broadcaster Jack Buck growled, "And we'll see you tomorrow night!" as Puckett rounded the bases. His walk-off home run forced a Game 7 against the Atlanta Braves in the 1991 World Series.

It was an unlikely World Series matchup, based on recent history. Both teams had finished last in their divisions a year earlier. They were the first two baseball teams to go from worst to first to meet in the World Series.

Kirby Puckett celebrates while rounding the bases after his game-winning home run in the 11th inning of Game 6.

11

Twins pitcher Jack Morris took the mound for Game 7 against Atlanta's John Smoltz. It was a classic pitchers' duel. The scoreless game went to the 10th inning. So did Morris, who set the Braves down in order, getting the final out on his 125th pitch of the night.

In the bottom of the 10th, the Twins loaded the bases on a double and two intentional walks. Pinch hitter Gene Larkin stepped to the plate against Atlanta closer Alejandro Peña. He drove the first pitch he saw to deep left field, over the head of outfielder Brian Hunter. Larkin raised his right arm high in the air as he ran toward first base. He knew he had just won the World Series.

The rest of the Twins streamed out from the dugout. Morris was jumping up and down, waving Dan Gladden home with the winning run. The 1–0 victory made Minnesota the winner of the worst-to-first World Series.

PERFECT TIMING

Kirby Puckett made two of the most memorable plays in team history in Game 6. Before his game-ending home run, he might have saved the game with his glove. With a runner on base in the third inning, Atlanta's Ron Gant blasted a fly ball to deep center. Puckett ran back to the warning track, timed his leap perfectly, and made the catch against the plexiglass fence.

GREATEST SHOW
ON TURF

The St. Louis Rams hadn't given their fans much to cheer about. The team had posted five straight losing seasons when it moved from Los Angeles to St. Louis in 1995. The trend continued in Missouri. The team's record got worse every season, finally bottoming out at 4–12 in 1998.

It looked like more of the same in 1999 when starting quarterback Trent Green suffered a season-ending knee injury in the preseason. But star running back Marshall Faulk and an unknown quarterback named Kurt Warner made the season magical.

Warner was a former arena league player who was bagging groceries while he waited for a tryout with a National Football League (NFL) team. He finally caught on with an NFL team, and by 1999 he was No. 2 on the Rams' depth chart. When Green went

Kurt Warner (13) attempts to pass around Tennessee Titans defensive end Jevon Kearse during the Super Bowl.

down, the Rams turned to the unknown 28-year-old who had thrown just 11 passes in his NFL career. But Warner surprised everyone. With his strong and accurate passing, he led an offense that came to be known as the "Greatest Show on Turf."

The Rams started the season with six straight wins and finished the year 13–3, the best record in the conference. Faulk topped 1,000 yards both rushing and receiving. Wide receiver Isaac Bruce caught 12 touchdown passes. Warner threw for 4,353 yards and a league-high 41 touchdowns. That season the Rams were held under 30 points just three times in the regular season and scored at least 21 points in every game.

The Rams were a 7-point favorite against the Tennessee Titans in the Super Bowl and jumped out to a 16–0 lead by the third quarter. But the Titans fought back to tie the score with just over two minutes left.

St. Louis responded quickly. Warner and Bruce connected on a 73-yard touchdown pass to put the Rams back on top 23–16. The Titans rallied again. But Rams linebacker Mike Jones dragged Tennessee receiver Kevin Dyson down at the 1-yard line as the clock ran out, and the Rams were finally champions.

RANKINGS
DON'T MATTER

Goran Ivanisevic watched the ball sail wide. It set up his third championship point on the grass courts of Wimbledon in July 2001. He bent down on the tennis court, folded his hands in a prayer gesture, and looked toward the sky. Ivanisevic was so close to his first men's singles Grand Slam title.

Just being in the final against Australian Patrick Rafter was a surprise for Ivanisevic. He came into the tournament ranked No. 125 in the world. The Croatian left-hander had already knocked off No. 4 seed Marat Safin and No. 6 seed Tim Henman to reach the final, where Rafter, the No. 3 seed, was waiting for him.

With the score tied 7–7 in the fifth set, Ivanisevic hit a pair of winners to break Rafter's serve. Ivanisevic pumped his fist in the air as the crowd roared.

Goran Ivanisevic receives a kiss from his father, Srdjan, after his thrilling victory in the 2001 Wimbledon men's singles championship match.

Then Ivanisevic served for the match. On championship point he delivered a serve that Rafter could only return into the net. Ivanisevic collapsed face down at Centre Court. He had gone from No. 125 in the world to Wimbledon champion.

The Boston Globe

SUPER PATRIOTS!

Capping a storybook campaign, they shock heavily favored Rams to become NFL champs

BIRTH OF A DYNASTY

The New England Patriots went 5–11 in 2000, just another disappointing season for a team with a long history of letting down its fans. But head coach Bill Belichick and quarterback Tom Brady didn't much care about history. They had arrived in New England in 2000. Belichick was hired to make the team a winner. Brady was a sixth-round draft choice who didn't start a game as a rookie.

But in 2001, starting quarterback Drew Bledsoe was injured in a Week 2 loss to the New York Jets. Belichick gave Brady the nod, and the rest is literally NFL history. The Patriots went 11–5 and pulled out two tight playoff victories to reach the Super Bowl, where they faced Kurt Warner, Marshall Faulk, and the mighty St. Louis Rams.

But the Patriots had one more surprise left in them. With the score tied 17–17 in the final minute, Brady led a 53-yard drive into Rams territory. Then Adam Vinatieri kicked a 48-yard field goal as time ran out. The Patriots had their first Super Bowl victory.

Wide receiver Fred Coleman celebrates the Patriots' shocking Super Bowl victory over the Rams.

QUITE A SHOCK

Putting together a championship team is like fitting together a puzzle. The Detroit Shock of the Women's National Basketball Association (WNBA) did a masterful job of it after a terrible 2002 season.

The Shock finished with the worst record in team history at 9–23, including an 0–10 start before hiring former Detroit Pistons great Bill Laimbeer as head coach. They took forward Cheryl Ford with the third pick in the draft. Center Ruth Riley arrived by way of the dispersal draft after the Miami and Portland franchises folded. Veteran guard Kedra Holland-Corn was part of a trade on draft day.

The Shock lost their 2003 season opener before rattling off an eight-game winning streak, just one shy of their win total in 2002. Their winning ways continued. Detroit eventually reached the WNBA Finals, where it faced the Los Angeles Sparks. The Sparks were the two-time defending champion and heavily favored. They won

Rookie forward Cheryl Ford, *right*, helped the Shock immediately with her strong defense and rebounding.

easily at home in Game 1. Back in Detroit, Holland-Corn hit a clutch three-pointer and Deanna Nolan made two late free throws to give the Shock a 62–61 victory.

In the deciding Game 3, Riley scored 27 points, and Ford clinched the victory with two free throws for an 83–78 Shock win. The celebration was on in front of their home fans. Ford jumped into the arms of her father, basketball Hall of Famer Karl Malone, in the stands. They embraced while a sellout crowd of 22,076 fans roared and danced.

The Shock had gone from 9–23 to a title-winning 25–9. Laimbeer was named Coach of the Year, Ford was Rookie of the Year, and Riley was the Most Valuable Player (MVP) of the WNBA Finals. Their team slogan wrote itself: they Shocked the world.

From left, Riley, Ford, Swin Cash, Nolan, and Barbara Farris celebrate after beating Los Angeles for the WNBA title.

BREAKING THE CURSE

The Boston Red Sox won three World Series from 1915 to 1918. The legendary Babe Ruth was on the roster for all three of them. But the Red Sox sold the young pitcher to the rival New York Yankees after the 1919 season.

That transaction launched the Yankees dynasty. Ruth became a full-time outfielder and set single-season and career home-run records with the Yankees. Over the next 84 years, New York won the AL pennant 39 times and captured 26 World Series titles. Meanwhile, the Red Sox went to the World Series just four times and lost them all.

Eventually, the idea arose that the Ruth sale put a hex on the franchise. Fans and media began whispering about "the Curse of the Bambino," suggesting that mystical forces were preventing the Red Sox from winning it all.

As his teammates pour out of the dugout, David Ortiz celebrates his 12th-inning home run to beat the Yankees in Game 4.

In 2004 the Red Sox made it to the AL Championship Series (ALCS) against the Yankees. New York had defeated Boston in the 2003 ALCS on a walk-off home run in Game 7. A year later, it seemed the Curse was alive and well as the Yankees won the first three games of the series. No team in Major League Baseball (MLB) history had ever come back from being down 0–3 to win a seven-game series.

The Red Sox chipped away. In Game 4, they tied the score in the ninth inning. Then slugger David Ortiz hit a home run in the 12th inning to win the game. Ortiz was the hero the next night, too. He homered to tie the score in the eighth inning, and his run-scoring single in the 14th won the game. Back in New York, Red Sox pitcher Curt Schilling shut down the Yankees, and second baseman Mark Bellhorn hit a three-run homer as Boston won Game 6 4–2. That forced a winner-take-all Game 7.

It wasn't even close. Ortiz got Boston started with a two-run homer in the first inning, Johnny Damon hit a grand slam in the second, and the Red Sox cruised to a 10–3 victory. They went on to sweep the St. Louis Cardinals for their first World Series championship since 1918. It took 86 years, but the curse was broken.

CAROLINA COMEBACK

t is said the Stanley Cup is the hardest trophy to win in sports. Teams have to survive four long, physical playoff series to become National Hockey League (NHL) champions. When they finally succeed, it's cause for a big celebration on the ice. The team captain grabs the silver trophy first and plants a big kiss on it before hoisting it over his head and skating it around the rink.

In 2006 that honor went to Carolina Hurricanes captain Rod Brind'Amour. He played in the NHL for 17 years before finally winning the Stanley Cup in front of the home fans. Alternate captain Glen Wesley was in his 18th season when he won his first Cup that year. He played in four Stanley Cup Finals and 169 playoff games before winning it all.

Carolina was a surprise champion. During the 2003–04 season, the Hurricanes had a weak offensive attack. They scored the fewest goals in the league and won just 28 games all season. The next year,

Carolina Hurricanes captain Rod Brind'Amour finally got to skate with the Stanley Cup in 2006.

31

the NHL canceled the season because of a labor dispute.

But Carolina turned it around thanks to rookie goaltender Cam Ward, who took over the starting job in the playoffs and led the Hurricanes to the finals against the Edmonton Oilers. Carolina took a 3–1 lead in games, but the series went to Game 7. Ward, just 22 years old, came up with 22 saves in that game. The Oilers didn't score until the third period. An empty-net goal late in the third period clinched a 3–1 victory for the Hurricanes. It was the first major professional title for a team in North Carolina, a state known more for basketball than for hockey.

RETURN TO GLORY

The Boston Celtics were one of the dominant teams in the early days of the National Basketball Association (NBA). They won 16 NBA titles over a 30-year span that ended in 1986. But the team fell on hard times after that.

After 21 years of frustration, the Celtics needed a change of culture, so they revamped their roster in 2007–08. The new faces delivered a turnaround for the ages on a team with no shortage of great performances.

All-Star forward Paul Pierce welcomed sharp-shooting guard Ray Allen and former NBA MVP Kevin Garnett to Boston. They had played a combined 32 seasons without any of them winning a championship ring. But that was about to change.

The Celtics went 24–58 the season before they picked up Garnett and Allen. They showed right away that fans didn't have to worry

Ray Allen (20) takes it to the hoop against the Lakers' Derek Fisher during the 2008 NBA Finals.

about a repeat of that dismal performance. Boston started the season with eight straight victories and won 20 of its first 22 games. The Celtics finished with a 66–16 record, the greatest single-season turnaround in NBA history. It ended with the Celtics in the NBA Finals against the Los Angeles Lakers.

The Celtics won the first two games at home and pulled out a win in Game 4 in Los Angeles. They arrived back in Boston with a 3–2 series lead and didn't leave any room for doubt as to the outcome of Game 6. Boston won 131–92, the largest margin of victory in a championship-clinching game for any NBA team. Pierce was the Finals MVP. Allen tied an NBA Finals record in Game 6 by making seven three-pointers.

Coach Doc Rivers removed Allen, Garnett, and Pierce from the game with four minutes left. They joined the giddy Celtics fans waiting for the championship to become official. When the final horn sounded, the players rushed the court while Garnett knelt to kiss the team's leprechaun logo at center court. It was a long journey for the three stars, but it was worth the wait.

RELEGATION
TO ROYALTY

A few good teams tend to dominate English soccer. The rest just try to hold on. Going into the 2015–16 season, Leicester City was in the latter group. The team from central England had been in the country's third tier as recently as 2008. Although the Foxes had won their way back to the Premier League in 2014, they needed a late surge to avoid being relegated to the second division.

So, coming into the 2015–16 season, Leicester's fans were more concerned with staying in the Premier League than winning it. After all, the Foxes came into the season as 5,000-to-1 underdogs to win the league title.

But a strong defense, with goalkeeper Kasper Schmeichel as its backbone, helped the team get off to a good start. And talented

Kasper Schmeichel (1) makes a save against Newcastle United in 2015.

Schmeichel places the crown of the Premier League trophy on the head of coach Claudio Ranieri as the Foxes celebrate their stunning championship.

striker Jamie Vardy set a Premier League record by scoring in 11 straight games. Shockingly, Leicester City had risen from the bottom of the league to contend for first place.

The Foxes took over first place for the first time with a win over Everton on December 19. In the second half of the season, they ran away with the title. They clinched the title with two weeks to play, holding a seven-point lead over second-place Tottenham Hotspur. Leicester City fans went crazy as they celebrated the most unlikely Premier League champions ever.

WHAT IS RELEGATION?

Many countries have multiple levels of soccer and other club sports. Teams move back and forth between the levels when they are relegated or promoted. For example, 20 clubs play in the English Premier League. At the end of the season, the bottom three are dropped a level. They are replaced by three clubs from the second tier—the first- and second-place finishers and the winner of a four-team playoff. Promotion and relegation take place at the top and bottom of every level of English club soccer.

108 YEARS

The Chicago Cubs have a long history of losing. By 2016 they had gone 108 years without winning the World Series. But fans had hope that the 2016 team would be the one to end that slump. Five Cubs pitchers won at least 10 games that season. Slugging third baseman Kris Bryant won the NL MVP Award. And the team got back to the World Series for the first time since 1945.

Then the Cubs lost three of the first four games against the Cleveland Indians. Could Cubs fans stand more heartbreak? And was "the Billy Goat Curse" ever going to end? The curse stemmed from the 1945 World Series between the Cubs and the Detroit Tigers. Chicago had won two of the first three games. Billy Sianis, the owner of the nearby Billy Goat Tavern, purchased tickets to Game 4 at Chicago's Wrigley Field. Sianis brought his pet goat for good luck, but officials asked him to leave the game because of the goat's smell. On the way out of the park, Sianis reportedly cursed the team and

Cubs slugger Anthony Rizzo blasts a home run against Cleveland during the World Series.

said the Cubs wouldn't win as long as the goat wasn't allowed in the park.

The Cubs lost that World Series and didn't play another postseason game until 1984. A few playoff runs fizzled out until finally the World Series skid ended in 2016. The Cubs rallied to win three straight games, including the last two in Cleveland. They clinched the title with a thrilling 10-inning victory, with Bryant throwing across the diamond to Anthony Rizzo for the final out. Curse or no curse, the Cubs proved that talent and patience can produce great turnarounds in sports.

BLACK CAT CURSE

The 1969 season looked promising for the Cubs, who had led the NL East Division by nine games in August. Then a black cat ran in front of their dugout during a game in New York in early September. The Cubs entered the month with a five-game lead over the Mets. In less than three weeks they trailed the Mets by five games and were sinking like a rock. They ended up finishing eight games behind New York, and their playoff drought lasted another 15 years.

GLOSSARY

ace
In baseball, the best pitcher on a team.

clutch
An important or pressure-packed situation.

dispersal draft
A process by which teams acquire players from other teams in their league that have folded.

dynasty
A team that has an extended period of success, usually winning multiple championships in the process.

favorite
The person or team that is expected to win.

franchise
A sports organization, including the top-level team and all minor league affiliates.

journeyman
A player who has played for many teams or has been unable to find a specific role.

knockout
A fight that ends when one competitor is physically unable to continue.

pennant
A symbolic term used in baseball to represent the championship of the American or National League.

walk-off home run
A home run in the final inning that wins the game for the home team, forcing the defense to walk off the field.

winner
In tennis, a shot that the opposing player cannot reach, winning the point.

ONLINE RESOURCES

To learn more about amazing sports turnarounds, visit abdobooklinks.com. These links are routinely monitored and updated to provide the most current information available.

MORE INFORMATION

BOOKS

Bryant, Howard. *Legends: The Best Players, Games, and Teams in Baseball.* New York: Philomel Books, 2017.

Campbell, Dave. *The Most Notorious Curses of All Time.* Minneapolis, MN: Abdo Publishing, 2016.

Wilner, Barry. *The Biggest Upsets of All Time.* Minneapolis, MN: Abdo Publishing, 2016.

INDEX

ABOUT THE AUTHOR

Heather Rule is a writer, sports journalist, and social media coordinator. She has a bachelor's degree in journalism and mass communication from the University of St. Thomas.